STEPHEN REID

THIS BOOK OF
SHADOWS & LIGHT
BELONGS TO

MY MAGICKAL NAME IS

Belinda J. Mörtz-Schmidtke

DEDICATION

This *Book of Shadows and Light* is dedicated to the reclaiming of magick. Every mark you make within it is a mark of dedication to your soul. When you make your mark within these pages, you will generate the courage to realise your potentials, the ability to create what your soul desires and the power to see how free and strong you truly are. I know you are capable of true, magickal things every day—the kind of things, that over time, weave together into an enchanted life that will not only allow your happiness to shine, but will change the world around you.

A *Book of Shadows and Light* is your own sacred, magickal journal. For hundreds of years, wise ones, magicians, witches and lightworkers of all kinds have kept personal journals in which they have recorded their soul-questing. Be it through meditation, inner exploration, mystic adventure, spiritual travels, magickal manifestation or blessed spellcrafting and casting, the uncovering of each individual enchanted path is full of unique wisdom. With this *Book of Shadows and Light*, you join these magickal practitioners in the quest to realise your soul's energy as it is meant to manifest within the world.

Within your *Book of Shadows and Light* you can write of the everyday moments of magick that you experience in your life. I've included images, chosen to fire your enchanted imagination, and words from my own *Book of Shadows and Light* to inspire you as you explore the mysteries of your own soul. Within these pages you can write up your spells and express your feelings about the process, the results and the craft of magick. (For example, you may wish to work with my Magickal Spellcards and keep a record of your results.) You can explore your dreams and the relationships you have in your life. You may wish to record your responses to the moon as she cycles through her changes and see how her shifts intertwine with your own. There are eight festivals of great magick within the Wheel of the Year. You can celebrate this cycle of natural magick of the earth and the stars here within these pages as you come to know the Wheel's energies and the festivals' impact upon you as well as your growing connection to your divine wisdom, self-knowledge and natural gifts of intuition.

Every *Book of Shadows and Light* is a place where you can explore your own experience of magick. This can be as private or as public as you wish it to be. There is a magickal law which is, "to know, to dare, to will, to keep silent." Within these pages, I hope you do all those things. Whether you keep silent—as in, keep your book for your eyes alone—is entirely up to you. But there is power in knowing yourself, and this can take time. So, my suggestion would be to keep your book for your own eyes, your own exploration, for a good while, while you begin the magickal rite of knowing thyself.

It is most important that your *Book of Shadows and Light* feels safe and your very own. In a very real way, a *Book of Shadows and Light* is a safe space, a world between the worlds, much like the magickal circle cast so often before spellcrafting, casting, rites, rituals and sacred ceremony. It is blessed, beloved and full of personal power.

The circle is a world between the worlds, a safe space within which you are protected and shielded as you share and as you seek. It is a sanctuary and an energetic temple dedicated to your own magickal practice. So too, this *Book of Shadows and Light*, is a holy space within which you are safe to discover your magickal possibilities, to know, to dare, to will—to become your own true self.

I wish you to know that you are a sacred being, full of natural magick. It is a magickal truth that the use of your *Book of Shadows and Light* will bring you closer and closer to the beauty, magick and wonder of your soul and to this beautiful, blue and green planet.

Blessed be, magickal one,

LUCY

LUNAR CYCLES

A wonderful way to connect with the lunar cycles is to explore them in your *Book of Shadows and Light*. You'll find inspirational quotes throughout these pages to help you explore and understand these energetic cycles, which have a profound impact on all of us.

The moon is a mysterious source of light and energy. Appearing to die and be reborn every twenty-nine and a half days, the moon is a symbol of renewal, change, magick, intuition and psychic powers, fertility, conception, pregnancy, birth and death. The goddesses aligned with the moon include: Selene, Artemis, Diana, Hecate, Cerridwen, and the beautiful Celtic goddess, Arianrhod, who governs the cycles of the moon, as well many other significant natural laws.

The full moon is associated with shapeshifters, such as werewolves, that are symbolic of how our wild inner nature can come out to play during the full moon when it is stimulated by the abundance of light. When understood correctly, the time of the full moon can be one of great beauty and magick. *The Charge of the Goddess*, a beautiful prayer attributed to the great twentieth-century witch, Doreen Valiente and also Gerald Gardner, considered by many to be the father of modern Wicca, says:

> *Whenever you have need of anything, once in a month, and better it be when the Moon be full, then you shall assemble in some secret place and adore the spirit of me, who am the Queen of all Wise Ones.*

> *You shall be free; and you shall dance, sing, feast, make music and love, all in my name.*

> *For mine is the ecstasy of the spirit and mine also is joy on earth; for my Law is Love unto all Beings.*

The moon is mysterious. Though there is much we do not know of her, we do know that her orbit of this planet governs the tides and interacts with the magnetic forces of Earth in such a way that everything here, all life on Gaia, is influenced.

The moon also governs the rate of growth of plants, which in turn impacts the magickal life of this planet. Fortunately, it is both natural and very simple to reconnect with the moon's magick to rebalance our psychic and intuitive energies, and restore us to our natural state—as powerful, healthy, loving, compassionate, creative and blissful beings.

Each moon phase, of which there are five, has great power.

DARK MOON

This phase of the moon is associated with going within. The dark moon is invisible in the night sky and this phase is about our own darknesses, what is unseen and that which lies within or beneath. It is associated with the old ones, the ancestors, the sage and the wise woman as well as the darkness that is the great underneath of the planet, the fertile soil and the depths of the oceans. It is the Dark Goddess—the ancient primordial mother who gives birth to us all. The dark moon is a time to let go of judgements about your so-called faults and flaws, a time of coming into maturity, a time of rest, repose, and of introversion and examination within. It is a phase of release, examination, telling your deepest truths to yourself and of peeling back layers. The dark of the moon gives us the opportunity to investigate the progress of your soul, to navigate the darker waters of self, for the truths of who you are without blame or judgement.

DARK MOON INVOCATION

Dark Moon, hear me! I release to you my fears, my secrets, and I acknowledge the lies I have told myself. I allow you to draw these from me, like toxins from a wound, and heal me with rest, acceptance and self-knowledge.

As you allow this healing to take place, this drawing forth to occur, you will feel a lightness, a sweetness and a peace settle upon and within you.

NEW MOON

After the dark moon comes the sweet, shining hope of the new moon. The new moon appears as the very slightest, shining silver crescent in the sky. You are now within a time of opportunity, potential and hope. This is the time to take the treasured hope and promise of pure possibility, and to plant those seeds firmly in your life.

NEW MOON INVOCATION

New Moon feel me! I plant within your silver radiance my hopes and dreams. I ask for your growing light to bless and bathe these new projects, my ideas and creations, and bring to them your energy and vitality. New Moon, I wish upon you, knowing what is meant to grow, will grow, and I will take action to support my dreams. In this way, they will manifest!

Whatever you wish for, this is the time to begin that quest. This is the maiden moon, the innocent, hopeful, optimistic new moon.

WAXING MOON

After the birth of the new moon, the moon will appear to be growing in the sky. Each passing moment sees her becoming brighter, stronger and more illuminated by the energy of the Universe and the star, our sun. The waxing moon's energy is about growth, nurture and change. Our ancient ancestors believed the moon was a woman giving birth to shining brightness. As the moon grows visibly larger and more powerful, it is time to allow our energies to do the same. The moon's growing light will shine its energy of maturity, growth, expression and solidity into your dreams... letting you intuit exactly what to do at any given moment to add life force and hope to your projects...

The moon is now glowing brighter, and she is growing, even as the misty clouds skim silver across her surface. There she is, in the night sky, nearly at her fullness.

WAXING MOON INVOCATION

Silver Lady, as you grow, may my dreams and projects too gather momentum, develop and mature. May I take all right steps in the direction of my dreams and may your silver light empower all that is for my highest good.

Your vitality is growing. Your power to change, make a difference and to manifest in the world is also growing. Allow the moon to whisper to you of creative ways to act on your dreams.

FULL MOON

She is glowing and so beautiful, and as she reaches fullness, you notice there is more life all about you. The plants and trees have grown. Your own body is aglow with her light. Your hair is vital and alive, your skin is shining and as she reaches the peak of her fullness, you can feel yourself filling with energy, happiness, and reaching a high tide in your own psychic powers, which are your natural senses in their most instinctual, vivid and alive state! You can sense and feel the world around you so clearly, and as you bathe in this light of the crystal full moon, her light sparkles through your every pore and into your cells. Her crystal light awakens dormant DNA that has the ability to create vibrant, glowing health and a resilient, strong self who can change and grow in the tides of life, in perfect rhythm with the Universe. Now is the time to see and celebrate your work and your intentions. Dance, make love, rejoice and sing out with friends, family and loved ones!

Wherever you are in the world, the moon is full at the same moment. See the universal bond we all have and feel the power of your life expand and manifest, and grow strong and shining too! You are alive and it is a great blessing!

FULL MOON INVOCATION

Full Moon, bless me at your fullness. May the love, the warmth of family of blood or family of spirit, and true self-love surround me, bubble up within me, thrill me, replenish me and comfort me in this nurturing full moon. I shall drink, drink and fill myself from your bright silver chalice!

Allow the wondrous power of the full moon to charge your energy with her silver light. Offer your joy to gatherings, ritual, or connections with those you trust and care for. Work with this energy to revive any stagnant or stale energy within you, and bathe in the bliss of her shining, ecstatic light.

WANING MOON

Now, the high tide of this lunar light seems to be slightly dying and indeed, we are entering the time of the waning moon. While the full moon is a time for joy and celebration of what we have achieved, at the very moment that the full moon begins to wane—to grow older, to die, to reduce visibly in size and shining brightness—the energy begins to be drawn away again. Now is the time to let go and release, to allow yourself to unfurl your hands and let go of what you have been holding on to, and to let the moonlight's power clear and declutter. Allow the moonlight to search throughout your life to find and collect that which may no longer be of any service to you. Sometimes this may be emotions, like hurt and resentment, anger and fear or disbelief in your own abilities, so allow the moon to scan through you to locate any unwanted or outworn energies you may not be consciously aware of. Allow the moon to clear this away, redistributing this energy, thus recycling it within the universal powers.

You can give further power to this gentle lunar action in your material life by clearing out an old closet; holding a garage sale; giving as a gift something that may mean a great deal to another, but little to you at this time; allowing a relationship which has run its course to dissolve and be complete; forgiving someone who you have nursed a grievance against; forgiving yourself for something you could have done better; and finding ways to free yourself from that which has been adding weight, disease, unease, fear or restrictions to your life. Each waning moon is an opportunity to set yourself free from habits that can be so hard to see clearly, and yet, be so destructive. It is a wonderful time to say goodbye to foods or habits, like smoking, which are not in your health's best interest. The waning moon is also a time to release behaviours like rage, gossip, complaining or an indulgence in negative thinking that get in the way of taking positive action.

Use this powerful time, which comes around again and again, to release whatever has lost purpose and energy, and prepare and recharge in order to move on. Take out life's garbage every lunar cycle and you will be astonished at what changes can be made, and what progress and brilliance can be achieved!

Timing important shifts and changes at work to this great natural cycle can see them come about more smoothly and easily. At this time your hair grows slower, the tides are smaller, and the moon's pull is detoxing the entire planet. Trying to grow something at the waning moon can prove challenging. With any new dream or project, you may be manifesting, think now of what can be winnowed, cut away or let go of. Cutting energetic ties between you and others is more easily and smoothly accomplished at this time.

As the moon diminishes in the night skies, the stars about her grow brighter, until we are hovering on the edge of the void of the dark moon once again, ready to go within, face our truths, rest, renew and emerge again.

WANING MOON INVOCATION

I ask for the blessings of the Waning Moon—I will create time to go within, and find, then begin to dissolve and transform those things that impede my progress towards self-love, and love and care for others.

With each of the thirteen great cycles we experience within a modern calendar year, we have unique opportunities. When we begin to link to the moon's cycles, then link those cycles to the great festivals and holy days of which we will learn of next, our lives become smoother, simpler, easier and more abundant. Life remains challenging, but we will have powerful allies to assist us, support us and help us become the magickal people we are.

As the night stars shine more brightly and the moon seemingly disappears into the velvet darkness, we too can go to our rest, know ourselves and love all that we are, for we are the cycles of the planet. We are born to experience this ebbing, this flowing, this waxing and waning, this fullness, this darkness and this rebirth, every twenty-nine-and-a-half days. May the blessings of the moon be upon you, within you, gently assisting you to release, to heal, and to create new dreams... every day.

And of course, record your experiences with the lunar cycle here, within your sacred *Book of Shadows and Light*. Begin recording your entries with the date, the moon cycle and the time of writing. This will give you a wonderful base to learn more about your own magickal cycles as you work with this sacred book.

THE WHEEL OF THE YEAR

There are eight great festivals to celebrate and observe within the Wheel of the Year. Four are of the stars—the solstices and the equinoxes—and four are of the earth, and are seasonal—observing times of growth, harvest, death and rebirth. In the old times, the Celtic people would observe days from sundown to sundown—a very different way of working with time. Likewise, the Wheel of the Year begins with Samhain, the festival of the ancestors, as it represents the 'sunset' of the light time of the year. The celebrations and rituals begin on the sundown of the first day and continue until the sundown of the following day.

Often our ancestors would stay up all night to honour a festival. This sounds easy at Litha when the sun is high and long and rises early, and even at Beltane, when the ancients would stay out all night celebrating in fields dotted with bonfires. But, they would also stay up at Yule, the longest night of the year, and keep vigil throughout the cold and snowy darkness to witness the return of the sun and the new spark of life. The people were as linked to and in tune with these important days as the earth was.

While the seasonal dates are prescribed, the celestial dates can vary by a day or two each year depending on the turning of the earth, its position in comparison to the sun and the cycles of the moon. You can check on the web, but keep in mind that you can celebrate as close to the actual day as is practical for you.

Celebrating the festivals in the modern world keeps us connected to the great cycles of nature and of the Universe. In turn, this continually renews our own personal magick, allowing us to receive, to give, to let go, and to create, over and again, in respectful, meaningful ways.

Personally, I think what's so wonderful and inclusive about solstice (and the equinoxes) is that these galactic events touch all of us—humans, plants, animals, the rocks, the stones, the sky and the universal web. A solstice or an equinox just is—it knows no creed nor colour and its energy is for all. The seasonal festivals may vary from location to location depending on agricultural traditions and climate, but they too are so inclusive—generally speaking, we all have cycles and seasons. I feel the Wheel of the Year is so beautiful because in its raw form it is absolutely non-denominational; because it celebrates and acknowledges natural phenomena and cycles. It's not 'human-made'—it is cosmic! We may celebrate it in ways that can be seen to belong to a particular spiritual system, but I feel the great truth underneath the solstices, the equinoxes, the tides and natural phenomena is that they interact with us all.

Indeed, merry solstice, to one and all! It is utterly inclusive to say so! It is impossible for anyone to be left out! And by celebrating this and similar events in meaningful, simple and respectful ways, I feel we will begin to heal the great separation humans have created between each other, between themselves and the planet, between themselves and the divine, between us and the nature within and without us.

Think of the festivals of the Wheel of the Year as portals into other realms or dimensions. They are days that are out of time and all have the unique quality of acting as a powerful doorway between the worlds. Although you can also access these realms on other days, the festivals are the simplest, most effective and most powerful times to draw back the veil and be a walker between the worlds.

Blessings to you, wherever you may be on the Wheel of the Year. May you feel Beltane's bliss, Ostara's fullness and beauty, the stillness and grace of the equinoxes, and the delight of the Summer Solstice. If you find yourself within the shiver of Halloween or its ancient mother, Samhain, move through and take a moment to remember its very serious, very profound roots.

——— SAMHAIN ———

Ancestors
SOUTHERN HEMISPHERE: APRIL 30—MAY 1
NORTHERN HEMISPHERE: OCTOBER 31—NOVEMBER 1

Just as a tree draws its energy from deep within its roots to gather the strength to flourish in spring, at Samhain we too draw strength from our roots, our ancestors, our memories, our past lives and ancient indigenous traditions. This festival is reflective, quieter and more about those who are not here in many ways. And we walk too between the worlds...

At Samhain, we acknowledge and thank our ancestors for the advice they can give us. We know that our ancestors from the past and our future descendants can walk with us at this time, and we respect their presence and their advice.

In the Celtic world, Samhain was held at the point when the sun became weak, and to our ancestors, a weak sun was a dying sun. Before its death, the support of the ancestors was sought, and sometimes given, on a day devoted to these Old Ones. The time of the weak sun was at a time we now know as October 31 — the day that has been consumed by the popular cultural phenomenon known as Halloween. The truth is, its roots lie back in our collective past — to a time that knew when our wise ones, our healers and all who have passed before us, gather together collectively. They have great wisdom and protection to pass on to us. Being beyond the constraints of life, the dead can see into the future. We knew they could help us — or harm us. So, we spoke to them, most days, but on one special day, we turned completely to them. We made their favourite foods, we prayed to them, we listened for their words and advice, and we took care to protect ourselves from those who had passed but were not yet peaceful in spirit.

———— MIDWINTER SOLSTICE / YULE ————

Rebirth

SOUTHERN HEMISPHERE: JUNE 20-23
NORTHERN HEMISPHERE: DECEMBER 20-23

May your hearth be warm, may the Yule log burn, may the Light be reborn, for the Wheel must turn...

Winter Solstice is a time for being with loved ones, for celebrating the return of life, for making wishes and asking for messages from the reborn sun god. It is a time to feel the first fresh rays of light on our faces. Even today, pilgrims descend into the great stone temple of Newgrange in Ireland to experience the first rays of the reborn sun cutting through the icy winter's darkness, like a sword of light and new life. The winter solstice is a magickal time of energetic reawakening — both symbolically in our lives, and literally, as from this day forward the days start to lengthen and things begin to grow again. It is a time when the dark half of the year starts to recede and the light half of the year is reborn.

If you find it difficult to motivate yourself or you think dark thoughts at this time, you may also be feeling the deep crone energy and her influence on the winter dark. But don't despair, soon the energy of the solstice will bring a lightening to your spirit and your energy, as the sun god and the maiden awaken across the land and within you.

This solstice symbolises the power of light gently transforming the power of darkness, and in reality it means the darkest days of the year are definitely over. It's a time for wishing, for regeneration, rebirth, hope and the promise of the true growth of projects that are dear to you.

—— IMBOLC ——

Beginnings
SOUTHERN HEMISPHERE: AUGUST 1—2
NORTHERN HEMISPHERE: FEBRUARY 1—2

Imbolc (or Imbolg) recognises the aspect of the Triple Goddess called the Maiden. It is the fresh, the young, the naïve and the new. You can approach situations and people with open eyes and open heart, and coupled with planning, this fresh approach to life can inspire your every moment to be happier and more energetic. After the dark, red crone energy of Samhain, the energy of Imbolc is blue and gold and young. This, by the way, does not mean you have to feel seventeen again. It's about rediscovering hope and newness, which we all need. It is part of the natural cycle and like a snake shedding skin, we can rediscover ourselves as tender, loving, beautiful creatures.

The feast of Imbolc is dedicated to the Goddess Brigid. It is a time when the world is renewed, when mother's milk flows, and so too your cup can be filled with the milk of Brigid. Open your hands, open your heart and feel them fill with her love and courage. Light your candle this night, welcome her home, feel her blazing truth and passion. Feel the return of all that nurtures and let the little ones come forth and be born—be they our own young, the young of our animal kin or simply the tender dreams of our lives. Brigid is bright fire; she is warm and loving. She is an arrow of fire, a grail of milk, a cloak of blue across all you wish to keep safe. Feel the energy of her sacred protection.

—— SPRING EQUINOX / OSTARA ——

Growth
SOUTHERN HEMISPHERE: SEPTEMBER 20—23
NORTHERN HEMISPHERE: MARCH 20—23

Ostara is a time of fertility and growth, and is dedicated to the Goddess Ostara. She is a fertility goddess and her symbols, the hare, new life and eggs represent fertility, spring and abundance. She resides within the land, the seed, the flower and the awakening spring—which was not called spring, but Ostara. Her hare can be seen within the fullness of the moon's shining face. The Venerable Bede, a dark ages historian, wrote about how the Northmen worshipped her and called her Eostre. They celebrated her with gifts of sweets, veneration of hares (who were also sacred to the British goddess, Andraste) and the resurrection of life observed in the form of the spring. This goddess had her origins, her symbols and her time, folded into the Christian observation of the death of the Christ known now as Easter. This is why eggs, chocolates and bunnies abound during the observation of the Christ's death and resurrection. (Eostrogen also derives from her name.)

I love gathering spring flowers to create a beautiful Ostara garland. I find such joy in the new blooms on the branches, in the feel and the smell of the vines and the tendrils as they spring to life! Ostara is a time to fall in love with the natural world and its gifts.

As an equinox, it is a time of equal day and night, and is the very edge of the tipping point into the light. After the spring equinox, the time of warmth and light grows, days become longer, and there is a sensuality and abundance to the energy all around us. Ostara is a time of balance, beauty, undeniable renewal and light—of being reborn.

——— BELTANE ———

Fertility
SOUTHERN HEMISPHERE: OCTOBER 31—NOVEMBER 1
NORTHERN HEMISPHERE: APRIL 30—MAY 1

Beltane is a festival of fertility, sensuality, pledges and passion. Its energy is a lusty call for true, deep love, for friendship's sweetness and for affectionate support. It is a daring, rich and exciting time, one in which marriages are celebrated and lovers unite by fires in the night. It is a time of sweetness, of honey and life. When celebrated, Beltane opens us up to our own potential for bliss.

Beltane is ingrained in the consciousness of our culture. Its disguises are manifold: spring fever, summer holidays, all night parties, fires on the beach, flowers in the hair, jasmine in gardens, lovers pleasuring each other in the deep of the forest, marriages in high spring.

The herds were purified by smoke as they were driven through a narrow passage between the Beltane ritual fires, which were laden with herbs and flowers of the fields. This smoke drove vermin and insects from the animals, freeing them from aggravation and leaving them free and well.

At Beltane, we marry, or as it was in the old ways, handfast. Handfasting takes its name from the moment in the ceremony, which was presided over by a wise man or woman and witnessed by the entire community, in which the lovers' hands were bound together with ribbons, cords or strands of vines and jasmine to symbolise their connection.

Oh Mother Goddess, queen of the night and of the earth

Oh Father God, king of the day and of the forests

We celebrate your union as nature blooms with bounty and hues

We anoint and worship thee.

——— SUMMER SOLSTICE / LITHA ———

Light
SOUTHERN HEMISPHERE: DECEMBER 20 — 23
NORTHERN HEMISPHERE: JUNE 20 — 23

For just a moment, Litha gives us a glimpse of life in all its perfection. It encourages us to seize the day, and to dwell completely in the magick of the present moment.

At the Summer Solstice, it is the time of the greatest light, the peak of brightness within the world. When summer solstice comes, the tipping point is reached. A death and a rebirth takes place with every solstice. Even at the time of greatest and longest light, we lose something. At every solstice, the dark or the light dies just a little in order for the wheel to turn.

When summer solstice approaches, the world can seem crowned in molten gold, as the sun pours forth a deluge of light. The wheel will turn, and turn again... Breathe, when Litha comes, be warm, be ready, be within her, alive again. Fill yourself with the radiance and magick of the light.

Litha is a time to be with loved ones, to relax into the warmth, to celebrate with feasting and friendship, and to acknowledge the fae, for this is their festival.

Be open to the energy of this time, as you gather with loved ones to enjoy and love each other. If you are alone at this time, connect deeply with the soul of the world. To every butterfly and flower, to the heavy fruit and the endless light, know you are not alone, but a beautiful child of the God and the Goddess. We're all cherished, and blessed to be alive at this enchanted time. Drink it up, open your heart, step into the wonder.

——— LUGHNASAD ———

Harvest

SOUTHERN HEMISPHERE: FEBRUARY 1—2
NORTHERN HEMISPHERE: AUGUST 1—2

At Lughnasad we tend to look back. We can feel pangs of regret for plans, dreams, ambitions and relationships that did not come to fruition. Feeling haunted by what we view as our failures can be overwhelming. It is wise to see any 'failure' as a lesson—to look back and learn is worthwhile, but to be immobilised by regret is not only pointless, it can be destructive. Not only that, it is short sighted to assume that you know what is and isn't destined to be a failure—only as the wheel turns will life's lessons be revealed. The energy of this festival demands that you plan and store for the winter ahead, create peace where you can, resolve disputes and harvest the bounty of spring and summer. We must then thank the earth and the Universe for what we have received.

You will notice the signs of Lughnasad in the lowering of the sun's arc in the sky, a stilling of growth, a slowing of energy and a need to think of the future while at the same time feeling reluctant to move on from the joy and plenty of Litha. At Lughnasad, in times past, a large wheel would be taken to the top of a hill, covered in tar, set alight and rolled down. Later called Catherine wheels (to hide their Pagan origins) for Saint Catherine, they actually symbolise the turning of the Wheel of the Year towards the dark. Ignite your own Catherine wheel at this time, as a reminder of time's passing, and the need to move on and think of what will be needed. Plan. Share some of your bounty with others. Leave a basket of fruit for someone who will appreciate it, give a donation, count your blessings and share them. As a sentient being, you have a link to every other being on this earth—give at this time, and you will be blessed threefold in return.

——— AUTUMN EQUINOX / MABON ———

Descent

SOUTHERN HEMISPHERE: MARCH 20—23
NORTHERN HEMISPHERE: SEPTEMBER 20—23

Blessings for this sacred time to you all, when the shadows and scythe begin to fall…

The bitter and the sweet collide at the festival of the autumn equinox, also known as Mabon (pronounced Mah-bon). Day and night are of (near) equal length, and—just for a long, blessed moment—all things are in balance. The autumnal equinox is a pause in the endless turnings of the wheel, and herein lies its blessings. This festival marks a time of peace, stillness and tranquillity before we begin the descent into the dark times. It is a time of readying and reckoning. It is the in-between, time-out-of-time before we must let go of the light. If you let this stillness enfold you on this day, you will find great peace within the quiet pause and truly feel blessed.

Mabon is a darkening time, but it is the dark of rest, of the womb, of the deep sleep in the long night. It is a time to bring in the wood for the fire, metaphorically or even literally, and to truly, seriously prepare for the colder time ahead. This great dance of shadows and light is a wonderful opportunity to look within, to give thanks for all that is good in your life, to understand the lessons that have been taught to you over the last turning of the wheel, and to prepare to give yourself space and time to enter the dark part of the year. Fix those broken windows, clear the fireplace, restock the larder, and repair the quilts and cracks in the protective boundaries of your home or aura! This is a time of rich depths, discoveries, contemplation, committed love and boundaries. It is an opportunity to strengthen yourself before Samhain, and the coming darkness of winter.

MINI GLOSSARY

Awen: A Gaelic word that translates broadly to divine breath or flowing inspiration. Awen is a term used within Druidry and Celtic-oriented magickal traditions primarily to describe an ecstatic state of grace. The origins of Awen lie within the faery realm and were transferred through to the human world through the story of the Goddess Cerridwen and her cauldron of inspiration.

Deosil: Sunwise. In the northern hemisphere, this is clockwise, as the sun rises in the east and moves to the south. Sunwise in the southern hemisphere is anti-clockwise—as the sun rises in the east, and moves to the north. This direction is expansive, opening, and a calling in.

Druid: Druids were the keepers of spiritual laws and customs within Western Europe and the British Isles whose power was vast prior to the Roman invasions and subsequent colonisations. They worked with their communities to impart restorative justice, conduct rituals, make sacrifices and read omens and oracles for the good of their people. Their skills were broad reaching and their training long and arduous. Today, the path of the Druid is undergoing a revival. The root of the word Druid is Duir, which has various meanings, including gate, oak and door. This is both a literal door and gatekeeper, and in a more mystical sense, the door or gateway into the unseen realms.

Geis: Geis is, very broadly speaking, a Celtic term that has to do with your life themes, taboos, boundaries and opportunities. It is different to karma, but Geis can be understood as a kind of Western Spiritual karmic process and teaching.

Ritual: A ceremony with an order and set structure often conducted with several participants. Magickal rituals are often held to celebrate the Wheel of the Year and its festivals, to raise energy for healing, or to create, experience and activate the sacred. If you conduct ritual, either as a solitary activity, or with like-minded others, you can write of this sacred ceremony within your *Book of Shadows and Light*.

Spell: Spells are intentional magickal acts often cast for a distinct purpose. They incorporate a clear beginning, middle section and ending. The energy generated by the spell and the spellcaster gathers and continues, moving and shaping reality long after it has been completed. Exploring your spells within your *Book of Shadows and Light* will assist you in your magickal practice.

Widdershins: Widdershins is to direct against the sun—the opposite direction to deosil. In the Northern Hemisphere, this is anti-clockwise—from east to north, to west. In the Southern Hemisphere, it is from the east, to the south, to the west, then to the north again. We cast circle or work or stir in this direction to clear, banish and separate, or to close or unwind a circle that has been cast for group or solo spellwork.

New moon! Time to make wishes and dream of all that could be. Bring in love, bring in peace, bring in sweetness, bring in wellbeing, abundance, creativity and freedom for all!

_____
_____
_____
_____
_____
_____
_____
_____
_____
_____
_____
_____
_____
_____
_____
_____
_____
_____
_____
_____
_____
_____
_____
_____

There are times to drink from the chalice or hold it to another's lips. There are times to touch the stone, to ground, to go to earth. There are times to fire up the wand, to direct its energy, to draw it down and sing it through. And there are times to draw the sword. This is one of those times!

I keep hearing and reading "intent is everything." It is not everything.
Intent is intent. Wed intent to action, commitment, knowledge and
speaking up... then you are on your way to a transformative process, be
it spell casting or changing your work, your home, yourself. Intent is
not everything. It is an honourable part of a holistic process. For your
reality to change, that process, most of all, requires your action.

You have a beautiful mind, a cauldron of wisdom... it is more free, agile, powerful, nuanced and creative than you have even begun to experience. Yours is an amazing, beautiful mind – please dance with it this day.

Never be too sure of the answers the conditioned mind is so ready to give. That is not your true mind. Your inspiring, flowing mind is the question, the untravelled path, the untold story, and yours alone to share.

The sacred is within the world, and within the rearrangement of elements called buildings. The sacred, when it calls, rings true as a bell through trees, stone, water and sky. Somewhere it will sing its magick to you today. Will you listen?

There are days when things are just so busy that I can feel my breath quickening, my heart rate climbing and the adrenaline beginning to flow. I welcome the excitement, the rush and the whirl, but when it gets just a little too intense – when I feel that scattering energy coming close – I take myself to my friends, the trees. The kind ones, the strong ones, the slow ones, the ones who support and hold, but who are full of truth and wisdom. My heart rate steadies. My breath slows and calm returns to the quick rush of day. I love you, my trees. And I thank you.

You. Yes, you – you bright, brave soul. Emerge a little from that dark place where you have hidden awhile. Let us see you again. Better still, let us see your light shine.

*Birth and death and beginnings and endings. All bring us to the edge
of ourselves and bring forth the core of who we are.*

When we work magick in a disciplined and directed way we enter a
stream of tradition and of natural energy, of ancestral wisdom and
knowledge from realms other than human.

Out of the darkness of the bud held tight, bursts the flower, searching for the light. I'll take hope where I can find it.

The best response to a curse? To thrive.

Beltane. Samhain. Bright. Shadow. Life. Death. Lust. Memory. Heat. Frost. Skywards. Below. Flowers. Roots. Creation. Destruction. All in this one world, this blessed planet of blue and green and all in between. Blessings for the ancestors, for the dead, for the ancients. Blessings for the urge to create, to lay down with your lover on the hot earth, and join the land to the sky so babes will be born. A blessing on your unions. A blessing on your memories. The breath of life. The cord that binds us all. Blessings to all, north and south, at this sacred time.

Early blue-sky morning and I'm tending the faery garden. Miss Spider's translucent gossamer net clings to my face for a moment or two. Message received: reweaving the web it is, then!

What you have truly, is what is within you. No matter how many readings, healings or channellings from guides you are given, nor the love, compliments, presents and glorious things you receive, when the sun goes down for the last time this lifetime, there will be you, what you chose to do and what you have developed within you. That is the treasure of your life, that is the quest. And you, your deep self, is the one mystery most worth seeking.

This radiant sky is the dying sun's last wish. Sol burns down amidst charred clouds of roses and coal-streaked cobalt. The lamp lit miracle called night begins...

You storm, you wild, sweet-smelling collision of cloud and sky and clashes of thunder! I ask you now – cleanse me, free me, wash me clean as I dance under the grey skies and dark rains.

The scent of a thousand flowers erupts about me. Eucalyptus underfoot, sweet
bursts of cleansing oil with each step. Frangipanis, honeysuckle, grevillea...
In the land of secret waterfalls and sacred lakes, delighting in the burst of full-
bloom life. May you be blessed, bright, and beautiful this shining day.

If you shift the focus from the self and train it on something greater – being of service, doing something kind, a mountain, the colour of clouds, making a change that will benefit many – something amazing happens. Consciousness shifts on a personal level. Happiness and bliss, even contentment, result. Today, shift the focus from what you call 'you' to doing something greater in the world. The result will be more personal happiness. THAT is magick!

We have become so attached to the idea of our body being a mere vessel of spirit, but the body is most truly an expression of spirit in material form. Disconnect from the body and you disconnect from nature, then from the planet. If we re-weave our beliefs about our total selves, the planet, animals and nature, the All-That-Is may begin to receive respect and love from all of us.

Do not tell me it cannot be done. More so, do not tell yourself it cannot be done. It can be done, if you want it done. It may require more than you are used to giving. More than you are used to doing. More than you are used to being. But it can be done, if you will it so.

I wish for you, the courage to realise your potentials, the ability to create what your soul desires, the power to see how free and strong you truly are. I know you are capable of true magickal things, every day. The kind of things that weave together into an enchanted life that will not only allow your happiness to shine, but will change the world around you, too. Three times three. Activate your power!

I have noticed message after message in this world telling me what to think, feel, eat, wear and do... and they have no power over me. I know there is a different source of wisdom. I trust my own inner knowing; in kindness; in magickal allies; and in guidance and information I respect and respond to naturally, like a flower turning its head to the light. Life is an amazing gift and I am grateful. I choose freedom, empowerment, optimism, kindness and magick.

The hardest choice you may ever face is saying no to a loved one when you know it is right for you to stay on your own path. When you love a friend, a child, a lover, you do everything you can to create affinity, but there are times when the only right answer for you is no. That is when love is tested and the true quality of the love shines.

When we can accept that another loves us, yet says no to us when it is right for them to do so, and it comes from a real, considered and true place, I feel we have reached a place of true freedom within our relationships. We have respect, and we accept, even if we do not agree.

I find intelligence, observation, wit, study and research exciting – and very magickal. When it is blended with natural craft and devoted action it becomes a very potent brew indeed. Awen itself perhaps?

For all those who have lost someone, whenever it was, whoever it was,
I care for your loss. It matters. Today I make offerings and prayers
for the souls who are choosing to complete the journey here on earth.
May we find solace in the whispered condolences of the trees, faith in
the Earth beneath our feet, hope in the blue sky. Let our tears join the
rain and sea and wash us clean again. Blessed be to all.

Let yourself feel, deeply, truly, with intensity… there is a time to shake your fist and roar to the sky. Let yourself crack open and pour out all of who you are. Peace will flow in and fill the space you've made.

_____
_____
_____
_____
_____
_____
_____
_____
_____
_____
_____
_____
_____
_____
_____
_____
_____
_____
_____
_____
_____
_____
_____

My greatest wish today? That we would learn and grow, rather than rush back into the comfort zone. That place where you are uncomfortable is the very place where your evolution awaits you. The very point when you expand and recreate, rather than replace and restrict... Too many souls bunker down and hold on to lovers, friends, creatures, themselves as they want to see themselves, maintaining a desperate life that broke apart for a reason... If your life is stretching, even breaking in some places, consider letting some of it die in order to recreate. Recreate yourself, your behaviour, your potential. Perhaps, when all about us falls apart, it may be time to grow into the space the broken places are making...

This morning I went for a walk. Nothing special. In many ways, it was just a walk along my city's streets. And as I walked, I found myself saying hello to all the plants and trees, and there are many in this part of the city. "Hello bromeliads... hello camellias... hello liquid ambers... hello jasmine... hello cycads... hello bird's nest... hello snowdrops..." With every hello, it was as if a thread of connection was woven between me and the world once again. And, that slight disconnect, that faint sense of being lost, began to shift and change. In its place was the world, saying hello back to me, thus winding my soul back into itself with threads of gold and honey.

When it comes to service and devotion, there is no first, no last.
We are all part of a tradition and we all have beauty to offer. Without
yours, the tradition is incomplete. Without mine, there is an emptiness.
Together, our service and devotions harmonise, and reach more, and
more, until the world is alive with song.

In one way or another, we all walk in the footsteps of those who have gone before. We all prepare the way for those who will pass this way again, in one way or another. This great circle of time and service is a great blessing. Wherever you are on this continuum, this wheel, this joining of footprints, making a fresh mark upon a well-trodden path is a holy rite. Much love to you, this sacred eve, as the night begins to flower.

If there is a person, or people, who seems to have a negative impact on you, it's best not to feel guilty about what to do. There are times when you simply must step away. It's not about who is wrong, or right, but about the disempowering impact. Of course, some of this impact may be experienced due to our own selves, as we all have insecurities, fragilities and vulnerabilities. This is unquestionable. However, when we continually experience a negative impact after being with a person, I feel it is intelligent to minimise the connection until we develop enough self-love, or enough strength, to be able to expose ourselves once again. Everyone's energy is not compatible all the time. Sometimes we can work through this, and the work increases our wisdom and development. At other times, it is exhausting, and a game, perhaps even futile. If you experience this, it may be time to decide to put that person in soul quarantine for a time. There is no guilt in this. It is what we must do at times, without blaming, excuses or tearing ourselves apart with criticism for our weakness. With love.

A dream can be as daunting as it is compelling. It seems to me that
this can be because we sometimes only acknowledge the big picture
and forget the quiet moments where we made the most progress.
A dream is realised through quiet, everyday actions of courage – and
this you can do, my friend.

So much change is created – alchemised – on a small, subtle level, every day. It's the way you accomplish, day after day, small and seemingly unimportant tasks that lead you to the greater shifts. It's those small moments that can reshape attitudes, reset mindsets, recalibrate energy fields and break open your heart. And it is those very treasures that you will rely upon when the large, unexpected, powerful changes burn like a comet through the wonder of your life.

See the magick in the small shifts you have made over the last twenty-four hours. Those baby steps lead you to walk in a new direction. And when you find yourself on the other side of the gate of change, know that it was every small promise you made to yourself and kept that helped you on your journey into tomorrow. Keep going. You're beginning to head in the direction of your dreams.

Motivation? It comes, it does, fleeting, wondrous, powerful. Dedication? Ah, she is there, every day, when you do the work, when you get up for your children, when you gather the firewood, when you pick up the paintbrush, when the words are written down, when you show up again and again, and do what needs to be done. Motivation? She is sister to the muse, and how could I not love her company? But Dedication... She is the one I revere, the one at whose altar I worship. Motivation inspires me. But Dedication has my back. Never await Motivation – simply be happy when she is there. Instead, make Dedication your Goddess, your compass, your guiding light.

Never let people steal your dreams. Never hand your tender possibilities over to the dream eaters. Don't allow yourself to be intimidated by people who suggest, even subtly, that they are better than you, know better than you, are more deserving than you. There are a thousand little cruelties that are spoken every day that are nothing but the verbalised illusions of the weak.

Build up an inner strength in your deep, deep self. Find those who inspire you, speak to your soul, who were or are courageous and marvellous, but who did not, would never, delight in asserting themselves through tearing others down. Find those whose work you find yourself feeling, that expresses something, says something that seems to unlock the shackles. Not so you can be them but so you can be like them – in expressing yourself, being yourself, knowing yourself and generously sharing yourself.

*True mentors will never attempt to shame you, or diminish your achievements.
They will say, go on, go on... you are so very nearly there.*

Find that sacred moment within your memory. Let its energy find its match within you and radiate it out, stronger and stronger, until your joy flows out from within you, drawing ever more towards you. Blessed be.

To Know
To Dare
To Will
To Keep Silent

When we moved from a connected form of spirituality that evolved out of the observation of natural cycles, to one that had a heaven, a hell, and all manner of protocols, we began to fear death. And death was a very real possibility to our ancestors, in the sense that it lived with them. We now try to deny death. We have made an evil of it and in the demonisation of death, we have forgotten how to live.

I have been through my own share of dark times – times when I have been drained or felt manipulated, lost and very alone, even betrayed... not only by outside people or forces, but by my own illusions, conditioning and by my own perceptions. There is no shame in this. It is our dark forest, and in time, we will dance within the light again.

I went outside for a moment, to do something very ordinary. And after the burdensome heat of the day the night was so fresh, and so lovely, and so cool and sweet, that I paused and let myself feel its enchantment. Right there, in the moment, there was nothing else. The air was an invisible sylph gliding past me, inviting me to lose myself in the dance with the scent of blossom, delicate and clean after rain. And suddenly I needed to be free, and to move, and to feel, and to open myself to the magick of the night sky and the sacred, potent stillness, to the dance of this night... This night that was full of dreams that survive after storms. Blessings to you, and may night's magick be yours, always.

A spell is Sacred Purposeful Energy using Love and Light

To open the heart, must it first be broken?

I am sorry to those who have felt their centre of love constrict, grow fearful or wither. I wish you to know love... love of self, love of life, love of survival, love of the moment, love of laughter, love of joy, love of nurture... to be love. To live within that energy. To become its expression, in your own unique form, once again, and return to the love you are.

How unhurt is your heart? Anahata... this is the sanskrit word for the heart chakra... to be unhurt of heart. There are acknowledged wounds of the heart, just as there is an ego which can be split and sent into distress. But there are many ways to be wounded. And to become again unhurt – unbroken - is a beautiful thing. To re-weave your own wholeness and to love your Self, with a beautiful love is a challenge for many. So riddled are we with woundings, and beautiful, even in our hurt.

Never think you must be perfect or unfeeling to be healed. The heart has its wisdom and its frailties. We learn through experiencing many challenges. If the heart heals, and regrows, then we are evolving the soul.

*I awoke, pulled on some clothes and went outside to take a lemon from
the tree. So hot, already... And the most-gentle rain, cool and sweet,
began to softly fall on me. A blessing, a cleansing and I accepted it,
my heart open. May you have the most blessed day. Be well, friend,
and may your hours be filled with good, simple things.*

I'm pondering whether I'm a seasonal learner. You know, it looks like nothing is happening, nothing's going on, but then suddenly, up grow the shoots and buds and leaves and finally, the flowers of knowledge. Or perhaps not knowledge, but wisdom... one fragile bloom at a time.

In every situation, you have an opportunity. We have all been hurt, let down, treated as we imagine we would not treat others. True magick comes from alchemising the base materials into gold. Take the pain and the hurt, and seriously look for your lesson. Perhaps it was not your fault – sometimes in life, there are truly unjust betrayals. But often, we hear what we want, see what we want and we play a part. I feel true character comes from a willingness to think on the lesson. On how we can evolve. And that is magick. To take the base material and create the gold of true character. We can all develop this. We just need to be willing to mine within.

If you can feel, you will heal.

If you can discover, you will recover.

To the east, the power, the wave, the flow
To the south, the storm, the wolf wind's howl
To the west, the land, ancestors, bone
To the north, the heart, the hearth, the home,
Before us the night, black bed of the stars
Tomorrow awaken, dawn's chorus is ours

There are many spellcasters, there are many witches. You bring your magick, your intuition, and you marry that with the natural cycles for a desired outcome. To me, this is spellcasting. The marriage of intent and action. The wedding of intuition and gnosis. Powerful, natural, effective.

Your every word a spell, your every step a ritual.

Until I am taken to that place, I know only what I imagine to know.
The moment of truth comes in facing the experience.

All witches work with cauldrons. Whether metaphorical or actual, you will work with one of the three cauldrons. One is inspiration. One is transformation. One is testing. Which do you work with now? And how do you work with this cauldron? You cannot avoid all three. But how you work with each determines who you are, and who you are becoming.

The silver bow of Artemis against the blue-black velvet of the sky...
goodnight, and blessed be.

And they all woke up. Some lived happily, others felt the pain they'd so long denied they had, but ever after, they were here. No longer hiding, or running, or thinking their way out of living. They woke up, and they lived. And whether happily or otherwise, it was forever after, and they and the world were all the better for it.

I adore the ones who find a way to express that ragged fragment of divinity, the jagged little shard of immortality within us all. Do not conform or polish yourself until all is smoothed away. Make your life a great discovery of who you are, from moment to moment, until you become, and become again, your many-hued self. In every moment, be your own discovery.

Anger – ah, now anger is a wild and misunderstood creature. Anger, when acted upon in purposeful, meaningful ways, can be liberating and truthful. Anger can create a cascade of events that lead to real, lasting change in the world within and the world all about us.

"If the time should come when you would fain have the love of some other man, then use this second bottle."

A spell is Sacred Purposeful
The earth, the air, the fire, the water,
To you I return, I am your daughter
Energy using Love and Light

Judgement and condemnation most often result in a kind of self-righteousness where people congratulate themselves for being unlike what they are often enjoying hating.

*Anger and meaningful action, create change. That takes courage and
the ability to know that we are all works in progress.*

I commit to becoming better than my doubts tell me I can be. I commit to being kind, to being of service, to being free, to being unfettered. I commit to living in grace in small ways, daily. This approach, unwaveringly applied, moment by moment, creates a richer, deeper life. May I be a good human, first.

You are star, and stone, and bud, and branch... may you and I have dreams that
bring wisdom's nectar to our waking lives... may we all be compelled to be a
little kinder, for a little longer, when we awaken to a new morning on this earth.

The more you insist on your imprisonment, the tighter the chains you've made will be. The more you revel in your freedoms, the more expansive your world will become.

Thought is magickal. Intent is vital. But action empowers.

Every action taken and word spoken today is creating tomorrow.
If you do the work today, tomorrow will unfold like butterfly wings.

Sometimes, something or someone, is exactly the right kind of wrong for you.

Make something beautiful from something left behind.
Do something unasked for, do something kind.
Transform painful feelings into reworked fields of light.
Understand the part we play, every day and every night.

Break your heart wide open at least once today.
Let the whole Universe feel who you are.

Live this day like an explorer in an unknown land.

Feel the newness of the world, touch the light.

We are the writers of the stories of our lives, and yet, over and again, the pen is passed from our hands, to another. Freely, we hand over the blood, the ink and the power, and say to another through our actions and our choices, "I am tired... confused... I feel weak... you write my story." No more. Today, take up your pen. Put down your words. Take your story back.

Everything you hide from the world is needed.

Let us be strong, loving, joyful and content. Let us look not to the world of illusions, but to our own imaginations and recreate the world in the shape of our truest dreams.

A few of the things I hear a lot: I'll do it when the time is right; I'm going to do that one day; I just haven't found the time yet. Guess what? The time is today. One day is now. Life is not going to hand those experiences to you and the more you get involved, the more you'll find. It's not about control, it's about participation – contributing. Being spiritual is not about being passive, flaky, vague or just drifting along. That's just not healthy or strong – and the planet needs you to be both.

'Fitting in' is one of the least worthwhile myths we have chosen to place our belief in. Most people, at their heart, have felt and experienced that sense of being the outsider. The people who explore that can become the great artists, musicians, explorers, lovers and creators of change.

Freya's tears, and Freya's Love... how often do we hear of her tears of gold, falling into amber? Wherever you are this day, or night, know that you need not be alone. For the Goddess resides within you, and outside of you, and she loves and cares for you.

Starlit dreams of wonder to you... may the deep rest, the healing slumber, the night's caress be yours till the sweet kiss of morning awakens us all.

My reasons to diminish myself are most often excuses – sorry things that my worst self manufactures to stay small and minimise the imagined pain of failure. I will not live that way. I hope you will not, too.

Although we wander, journey far, remember, always, who you are.

Ameratasu is a goddess of rebirth from the darkness and she is profoundly influenced by flowers. Her story reminds me that when we lose our flowers – or our connection to nature – we grow profoundly sad. When one destroys that connection or when we allow it to be taken from us, by our culture, by our work, by mechanisation and soullessness, we too become profoundly soul-sick. We, like her, go to that cave. Ameratasu's story is one of spring after winter, but also of recovery after great soul-sickness due to a loss of connection from the natural world.

*If you wish to reach the beating heart, the truth of yourself, there is no
need to find the flaws in others and shout out the contrast. Only see
within. Look deeply and know who you are becoming. Live from that
place. Life will be rich and for the most part, life will be good.*

There is a massive lifting of the veil taking place. Only, it seems to me that it's the worlds within us, in our very souls that are revealing themselves. It's like I can see further, feel further – my senses are being stretched. I am not sure I can take in all I am being shown or feel all I am becoming. Hyper-sensitive, but strong at the same time... my heart is so very wide open. It has its own eyes and can see and hear. Something profound has changed, yet it is so subtle it cannot be named.

Something lovely seems to be twinkling on the horizon.

Something bright and lovely is most definitely twinkling on the horizon!

There is no greater day than this one to be fully alive and committed to my path.

During this beautiful day, I had a moment of anxiety, where I felt energy that could not be unfelt. So I went to a kind, welcoming tree, asked permission to enter its space, stepped forward and just stood within its green circle of peaceful, slow energy – breathing, deep and slow. My in breath, drawing in the out breath of the tree. The tree, breathing in my out breath. In that way, the moment of anxiety transformed. It did not end or leave. It wasn't over. But it changed. I changed. Thank you, tree friend for your green healing. May the blessings of the trees be with you.

Saying something grand with great certainty, as loudly and often as possible, does not make it true. It may make people who are less certain give their power away to this personality programming, but it cannot make it true, honest or even what that person authentically believes. Force does not equal truth.

A charcoal sky bruised by a slow-brewing storm. Golden candlelight. A heart like a cup, overflowing. Love and blessings to you this night. Be well. Sleep deep and peacefully. Know you are loved.

We will live in freedom. We will love who we choose. We will not suffer false structures to shame us. We will not be chained by your dogma and judgement. We will be free. Your time is ending. Ours is being cracked open, our power mighty, the energy explosive. All you have done to hold us down has strengthened us. Watch the world change. Watch us rise.

Deep breath... End of a simple, busy, good day. Breath out... Feeling myself readying for sleep, deep and peaceful, in the arms of the goddess that is this dark, blue night. May we all return from her embrace healed, whole, vital and shining.

So much understanding deepening – allowing me to make much more fruitful choices. It is sad to let some things go, but ah! The lightness of telling the truth. And I do mean the truth – deeper than an opinion or a reaction or a belief. A truth brought about by observation and awareness. And by taking responsibility. Blessings, friend. Much love to you this day and night.

When you let yourself feel - really feel – it is not always a 'pleasant' experience. But I would offer that it is nearly always worth discovering what you are truly holding within you and letting out any pain, anger or unfelt grief in ways that are healthy and robust – or gentle – and real. Too many people, so full of unacknowledged emotions, blame and hate, act out and inflict wounds every day. Know your own feelings and do the best you can to know what is yours and to heal it, if you wish, a step at a time. Take it easy, but do be authentic. No matter how much you would rather be 'nice.'

It seems to me to be a kind of crime to encourage victimhood, to insinuate others embrace their weaknesses and pity themselves and condemn the world. Each day you have the potential to change. Each moment you can choose. When you receive advice that disempowers you, closely regard the source. Learn not from those who are noisy, reckless and greedy.

Sensitive people, it's time to assert yourselves. Speak up. Show up.
Ask for the changes you long for. No more hiding away. Starting now!

Sweet Night, take us to a deep rest, let us journey and dream our other lives, let us meet and gather, let us restore and replenish, and Mother let us awaken to morning's kiss with gladness and thanks in our hearts. Good night. Sweet Night.

Liminal spaces are the keepers of magick – gateways where world touches world. Today I drew rune wishes into the sand at low tide, waiting for Sea Mother to carry them into the cauldron of ocean.

*There are times when you get such a short, sharp and sudden shock
that all the world recedes, and all you can see and feel is what is truly
important. It is hard to be grateful for this – yet, I am.*

That which makes you a misfit is exactly the thing the world needs right now.
Your weird is what the world needs to evolve and heal.

May your every moment be blessed. You are everything you will ever need. You are the answer.

My wish is for you to feel connected to the sacred, to feel loved, to laugh and share – for our time together in this lifetime is always brief.

*Remember, without anger, we can remain unmotivated – harness it,
use it, and ride its wave of power to put an end to a situation you have
put up with for far too long. Then let it go, or it will turn to illness and
bitterness. If you use it wisely and do not abuse it, it will be powerful!*

When you change, you do not have to despise who you have been or who you spent your time with. Nor do you have to disrespect them or yourself for the choices you made. Nor do you need to look down on those who are currently experiencing what you feel you have transcended. I feel we are all on a wheel. We revisit the themes of our life, again and again. We make the same kind of mistakes, only we deal with them in wiser ways, and we encounter the same people, albeit in different guises. This is because we are continually working through the geis of our lifetime. We grow, we adapt, and sometimes, we do better. That is a rich source of feeling good about who we are and what we choose. Those who feel better about themselves by continually comparing and assessing others, are often those who are the most stuck in their themes. Geis then becomes their curse, as you cannot work your way through your own evolution by continually comparing yourself to others in order to find the worth in yourself. You can only measure your evolution by who you have been, who you are becoming and by the small, sacred actions you take each day.

Take a deep breath in and just feel whatever it is you are feeling... no pushing, no perfection, no prodding at your tender self. Just a deep breath in, a blessing from the trees. As I breathe in, there is eucalyptus and the scent of good earth, and rain gathering on the hills behind my family's home. As I breathe out, I offer to the trees my thanks and a pledge to love myself, just as I am, just for this moment. And that will be enough for now. May this moment of self-love and acceptance be enough for you too, this day.

Sing your soul-song this day. Pour the true essence of yourself through your energy, within your voice and into the world. You will have an impact today and you will change someone's life. Let's co-create something beautiful together.

We are advised to go and love someone, just as they are, and then watch how beautifully they transform. Today, I would suggest respectfully that before we do this, let us take that same wisdom and apply it to ourselves. Love yourself, just as you are. And watch yourself transform.

Life is a dream with eyes wide open. Blessings of the day to you,
wherever you are dreaming on this beautiful green and blue planet.

When you have never met, yet your souls know each other...

From this sunset, this liminal time and space, I can sense a circle of souls, ever open, unbroken, eternal... Goodnight, friend. May dreams find you well, treasured and beloved this evening.

You are very beautiful, all of you, spirit, form, heart, the whole messy bundle of things that make up who you are.

Things fall apart. We come to pieces. We live.

The most beautiful sunset I have seen for some time – the wide, high sky streaked with coral and violet, shimmering and vibrating like molten gold. It was so alive and textured and the sky had depth – colour layered upon colour, shifting and changing moment upon moment. A kaleidoscope formed by nature. And now it has softened to velvet, stars writing in light across the inky purple of falling night. I cannot help but feel blessed.

A memory. A little moment from a long time ago for this witch. Late twenties. Finding my way, a little deeper along my personal path. Reading cards. Dreaming of creating oracles. Scribbling in notebooks. Lighting candles. Staying up far too late. Climbing trees at dawn. Loving the wrong people way too hard. Dreaming with eyes wide open. Feeling way, way too much at times. Open to the mysterious, ready to be... be whoever I was meant to be. I often speak to my older self, when I need advice. If I could go back now and talk to this young woman, this witch, it would be to say you will be okay. Don't be afraid. Keep being brave. You are becoming.

As the moon swells and fills her silver self with energy, so too will we all feel a little brighter, a little wilder, a little stranger as she reaches her peak. Last night the silver lady flew high over the mountain, clearing the forest, sailing free in clear skies. And I gazed and gazed and drank her in. Dew beneath feet, arms to her light, eyes to the sky. May your day be most blessed, may your energy feel free and joyous, and may your feet find the earth soft and kind. Dance in this energy, and feel its sweetness free you!

There is a time to sing and time to take up the sword.

*We washed away the old and stuck, beneath the drenching
starlight, then skyclad we smudged the space. Then we witches lit
candles, sang out our wishes and danced and whirled in the new.
Awake, and arise! It is a new day!*

It is beautiful to be touched, even set alight emotionally... But the fire and passion must change us in ways that alchemise our best possible selves. Be gentle with yourself. It's early days on your soul's road.

Sitting, drawing up the love and calm of Mother Earth to centre and ground me before I embark on a day of readings. May there be so much kindness within your day. May this time of light be good to you.

Let your true self shine out this day. Let unspoken words fall from your lips. Let your eyes share secrets. Radiate your energy into the world. Contribute a blessing with every breath, every heartbeat.

One still moment before we enter the slipstream of events, thoughts, conversations, interactions and connections. One long, still moment between you and the Divine. One still moment to remember who you are, to breathe deeply in and to let the breath go, in a cycle of three. You are divine.

Life's harshest moments are like ancient initiations. We are torn apart in the crucible that is birth, or the break-up, or the betrayal. And then, we slowly reconstruct ourselves in almost every way into faith, and love, and reborn hope, and trust. All these hurts are deeply transformative and beautiful, in a very primal way, and agonising too – as close to death as we can come, without leaving. Therefore, they are the keys to our own rebirths.

When I have a question, I turn to the wise old ones within the oracle
cards. The Dragonfae, the Faery, the Mermaids. You can do the same.
Bring your question, and ask their advice. Then be ready to receive
their counsel. May we find the clarity we seek.

As we dream, another world awakens in the darkness...

*Dreams are the human flowers of the night... the gardens of our souls'
bloom in the darkness.*

I love learning from the library of trees. Today I went to them again.
Natural magick and synchronicities abound.

One still moment before we enter the slipstream of events, thoughts, conversations, interactions and connections. One long, still moment between you and the Divine. One still moment to remember who you are, to breathe deeply in and to let the breath go, in a cycle of three. You are Divine. May you have the most blessed day. Be well, friend.

Take a deep breath and pause, before letting it all out. Three times the charm, three breaths the doorway into centring and calm. If a day of fast energy is ahead, take a moment throughout your day to pause, breathe deeply and re-centre deep within your being, the place where all is well.

Tree beings are among the kindest and most loving of all the elementals.

I have a lot to learn, as an ever-evolving human being. I am always learning, in every moment. And I resist learning too, very much so, and usually when it's what I most need to learn. But I am committed to being aware and that is tough at times, because I need to focus on what I need to learn. I ask myself, "How can I do better?" I want to be conscious of my woundings, awake to my sneaky triggers, to take responsibility for myself and develop healthy relationships that are not toxic hotbeds of intertwining damage. I am always learning about boundaries. How to ask for what I deserve, without falling into the role of victim, or feeling guilty, or afraid of rejection for simply saying what I deserve. I think I'll be working on that for a long time, and that's okay.

I am noticing a change in myself. I am experiencing not being afraid to speak up, that it is okay to be very straightforward, and that no matter how tough someone has had it, it is never okay for them to use that to manipulate and justify their behaviour. Never.

I'm taking fears and replacing them with fierce.

Taking good care of yourself, asking questions about how things will work and making sure you are not putting yourself at risk financially are not signs of 'ego.' We need to be good to ourselves and it is much more than okay to be both magickal and assertive. I love working with people who are straight up, who are grounded and strong, as well as loving and magickal. We can be all. Time to end the belief that caring for ourselves is somehow unspiritual.

Birdsong, blue sky and a shimmer of fresh energy. We're moving again. We're back in the flow. I'll give thanks and take another step into the bright unknown.

I love the place where intuition, natural inclination and skills, and book learning meet. I have so very much to learn. I have been so inspired by those who have gone before – so I visit ancient places, forage in museums, learn crafts by hand, open ancient texts and listen to the old languages while I watch, dream, experiment and keep on wondering, keep on learning... There is a history and a story to this craft. We are stronger and our practice is more grounded when we honour them.

To frost and flowers, from bone to flesh, from womb to grave, from the cry of life to the soft release into death and from beds of moss we shall rise.

You are like a butterfly within the cocoon – pushing, writhing and working your way through some kind of barrier. Green blood pumps through your fragile wings, making you strong and ready to emerge.

Change seems to be coming to get me – and while I move and shift within, something outside of me seems to be reaching for me, just as I am beginning to reach out.

I feel like I am shaking myself awake, stirring, regaining clarity and feeling fresh emotional energy, excitement, anger, impatience, and a sense of raising my standards. I refuse to comply to demands. I won't be a spiritual stereotype.

I want to break open and break free. I don't know what is taking place. I don't even know where I am going. I am cutting through cords and unbinding myself. I must live fully, fearlessly, and I must change. I feel I've been resisting this, unconsciously, for too long. Now, I am beginning to be ready. My energy is stirring. I can feel the fire within again. And I am excited. Rebellious. Unsure. Unbound.

Let's dream a while and find our tribe amidst the rich labyrinth called darkness.

*I passed a fountain where water flowed forth for a village and it felt
blessed and beautiful to me. I was just walking by, but I paused, and felt
something stirring in its presence. May we have the blessings of water
this day and may our thirsts be eased by its sweet gift.*

Today, I'm going to put these wings of mine to the test. What will you do to live just a little more free and true this day?

Oh, Moon, allow my cup to be filled, again and again, with what my soul needs, dear Goddess of the Silver Wheel.

You let me set free what was caged within.
Softening, the soul begins to sing.

No list can ever describe the unravelling of your losses. From friendships to family, endings, transformation, rejection, betrayal and just the unexpected sideswiping of gentle hopes for a future. We feel a little mad at times from the hurt of it, drunk on our heightened sensitivity. There are great, torn places in our lives and we have no real sense of what will fill the gaps created by the loss. Yet we go on. And, in the most surprising moments there is sweetness and peace. It is painful, but not without its strange bliss. We ebb, we flow and we continue, grateful amidst the madness of it all. This is life, in all its beauty and wild, stormy glory. We are alive.

Sweet night, take us to a deep rest, let us journey and dream our other lives. Let us meet and gather, let us restore and replenish, and Mother let us awaken to morning's kiss with gladness and thanks in our hearts. Good night. Sweet Night. Blessed Be.

*Let us plant the seeds of dreams on
any new moon night. Write down three
dreams to grow three tender wishes
of your heart. You may wish to create
a place, a space in your heart, an
experience of another land to reclaim
a part of your soul or a deep healing
of the body, the mind or the spirit.
Speak these three aloud, one after
another. Finish off with a little chant
to seal the spell and give your wishes
that extra charge to bring them to life.
Perhaps something like this:*

*By the power of three by three
I ask these wishes now to be
Grown and offered up to me
By silver light, by new moon bright
Bring to me what is good and right
By the power of three by three
As I do will, so mote it be!*

*Tend to your three dreams,
offer them support, patience
and action, and they can be
brought into the fullness of life.*

Find some space and time with kind humans who do not rush or speak to fill the space, with the elements, with the wild ones and with the tender and beautiful animals. Separate yourself for a time from the clamour and the din of ego and competition, and sink into the rich wisdom of the earth. Lie upon a bed of wildflowers, plant seeds into good earth. Slow down a little and hear the song of the world, within you, within the trees speaking...

This pain will pass. You will knit yourself together again. And, as your renewed energy begins to dance within you, so too will your soul be free and you will be whole again. Be gentle to yourself today. We all deserve respect, kindness, and generosity. May the deep peace of nature be yours this day.

Just imagine, that the thought you have right now, in this moment, will become your reality. What thought will you choose? Your every thought is a spell, working its magick. Choose wisely and create a life of wonder.

Convention can be extremely harmful. The desire to be accepted and embraced by the culture we are in can override exactly the things we need to do to create health, bliss, love and wellbeing. I have witnessed over and over how the desire to belong creates the perfect conditions for illness, unhappiness and people limiting themselves, fearing being different, hesitating to even take care of themselves. Please, good people of the planet, choose your tribe. Choose the tribe who wants you to be well, and loved, and loving, and part of the planet.

Rise and meet the light of the morning with the light within you.

How do you enter this Circle?
In Perfect Love and Perfect Trust

_____
_____
_____
_____
_____
_____
_____
_____
_____
_____
_____
_____
_____
_____
_____
_____
_____
_____
_____

A chant to cleanse your home. Move about your home widdershins,
clapping gently but firmly. Chant out loud:

Out, out and from within
Cleanse this space from trouble and din
Out, out, let all be gone
And make this place a cheerful home
Cleanse and clean, creatures in-between
From dusk till dawn, ensure energy is reborn
Leave it clear, and bright and blank
For this task, I offer thanks
Now please wish me well in this
May all brought in create my bliss

I am the dancer that moves through the fire, who wields my sword and severs the cords of energy that entangle you. I am not afraid of the death that needs to take place, for every act of destruction is an act of creation. I will clear all that drains you this day and bring you to new life on wings of fire.

The old world is gone, and the new world is yet to be found. So trust.
Trust and follow the compass of your inner guidance.

We need, for times in our lives, teachers. And a teacher, a guide, a mentor will soon be within your life. They are here to help you find the way while walking your own path, for there are times when all seems dark about us. Let them light your way awhile and nourish the new connections that will grow as you learn.

There can be no more delaying. The change has begun.

You have received clear, definite signs, answers to the questions you ask, again and again. Today, it is time to see what has already been shown to you, to listen to what your intuition has shared with you and to take action – without any further hesitation. Follow the guidance.

By acknowledging your truth and giving everyone about you the
freedom to be honest, everyone's light can shine more brightly.

*When you connect with your soul's truth, just as it is, now, there will be
side-effects... Speaking up. Laughing out loud. Saying no. Saying yes.*

The soul knows what it needs to heal itself. You need only listen to its whisper.

The rain is tapping its fingers at the windows, drumming nature's rhythm on the roof. Reading tales of ancient magick by candlelight, sleeping wolves guarding the bed, my love asleep, my child safe and warm... This is my world as night's high tide glides in on black wings. Closer and closer to midnight, to the witching hour we go.

Do you remember the times when you played with the faeries at the bottom of the garden? Do you remember when your friends, the invisible ones, were more real to you than your own parents? What of the first time you glimpsed your own shadow, quivering in the light? You seem to have momentarily forgotten all the precious moments, blessed one. Today, they will be returned to you, so your sadness can be transformed.

Do not hold on so tight to what you believe makes you, you. Let yourself change. Be recreated – renewed. Don't tell yourself again and again who you are. That is who you were. That is your memory of yourself. Something new is stirring and will break through, if you permit it. You are now becoming and who you will be is the sweetest mystery.

In order to live, we must learn how to die. To die every day to the things that do not serve our heart, our soul. To let go, to release, to clean and clear. We must all do this, again and again. Die, die, die, and then rise, rise, rise, into the life reborn.

You are on the verge of a new day. It is from those delicate and faint beginnings that something bright and strong will grow. Do not dismiss the tender signs. They are the seeds of your own new life.

All is well.
All is well.
All is well.

For my law is love unto all beings…

I just finished my active day with a naked swim as the last rays of sun pierced the sky with molten swords of coral and scarlet. The moon's silver, shining quietly above me, skyclad, alone, immersed in saltwater, with skin feeling so completely the water, the air, the breeze. I feel blessed. Be well, friend. Sleep peacefully and may your dreams bring you every blessing. Goodnight.

It's a soft grey day and I can sense the spirits of my northern ancestors in this mist, the soft rain, the low clouds shrouding the sky. I can feel Avalon rising. So, as the veils thin, as the moon swells to full, and the wheel turns, turns, turns again, may the mists protect us all...

Diarmid & Grania in the Quicken Tree

When the dark moon comes, the mirror of shadows is ready for you to gaze within. This night is for letting go... looking below... taking it slow.

"Dance as I rise," she said...
Lady Moon and I, this night...

Sometimes, I feel overwhelmed with gratitude and elation for the gift of being alive. To have been able to see the fog, moving through the light, vanishing until pure blue, framed by red-leaved trees. That's my revelation. That's my book of law. I feel I just saw winter's arrival, and it's in the re-seeing, really seeing the world, and its beauty that I'm lifted up so high. It's magnificent and simple. My perception has been cleansed by one small walk on my street – the red leaves, the swirling fog, the streaming sunlight. One sweet conversation with an elderly lady, who is going to a funeral today. One moment where I saw the tendrils of fog gather and lift, as though it had decided it was time to depart. It felt sentient. And the sky, the blue sky, returned again with the light of the sun. Re-see the world today. That is the great adventure. That is the purpose.

Drowsy black butterflies pass me by, the trees so heavy with mangoes
their branches kiss the earth, frangipani blooms carpet the green, and
even the rain-filled clouds seem benevolent, relaxed and kind. For this
moment, all is well. Thank you.

I had a transcendent kind of moment. I felt something like grace, and was suddenly aware of a feeling of gratitude that just naturally, strongly welled up within me, flooding my awareness. And I wanted to say thank you.

*Gathering spring flowers to create a beautiful garland. It's such joy to see
the new blooms on the branches, to feel and smell the vines and tendrils
springing to life! I am in love with the natural world and its gifts – so
generous and lovely, so delicate and sweet!*

A healing ritual bath with essential oil of lavender, a handful of consecrated salt, hot water and beeswax candles ignited with light. The bliss of bathing is in the alchemy of flowing water, molten golden fire and blessed oils. Liquid light and heat and scents... Treat yourself as the sacred being you are.

Today, I am so grateful for restoration, for justice and her blade of truth! I am grateful for the wisdom of plants, the companionship of animals and the joy of having people who love me, to love right back.

Today, just do you. Don't worry about that person over there, doing their thing, or that person over there, doing their thing. Don't worry about being behind, or ahead, or too this or too that. Don't worry about how you're not as *fill in the blank* as everyone else seems to be. Just do you today. Whatever that is for today, you be it, embody it, ensoul it, live it right from the inside out. Don't waste your precious gift of a life turning your beautiful head this way and that, giving yourself a headache over who's doing what and why you're not this or that or the other thing over there. It's exhausting, corrosive and not even the point. You're here. You have some things to do. And whatever that thing is, and however it looks today, just focus on you. Let your soul sing out through the quirky way you've done your hair, or written that line, or painted a stroke, or washed those dishes, or danced or skipped or walked to work or sung on the bus or smiled randomly at puzzled strangers whose day you just made. Stop all the worrying. You're not here to do that. You're here. You're so amazing. Take a moment and just feel that. And then do you. Shine bright like a light that will never go out.

The fires spoke with flame and spark
Oracles shared 'neath moon at dark
Stars burned runes in skies above
Three witches joined in power and love
Blessed dark moon to you, friend...

My spirit created a body, and thus, it is worthy of my respect and love. My spirit sang, and a body came forth. It is a blessing to be here in physical form.

The soft grey sky is full of white, sulphur-crested cockatoos and corellas in full cry. They come in annual cycles at summer's end, and it seems the air cools and autumn days wait for their arrival. I love this time of year. I love seeing wild creatures eating from the trees on the city streets, spitting seeds on the cars, their sonic call splitting the air, waking us up to the wild!

THE CHARGE OF THE GODDESS

Traditional attributed Doreen Valiente and Gerald Gardner
Adapted by Lucy Cavendish

Listen to the words of the Goddess, she of many names

Astarte, Inanna, Artemis, Aphrodite, Brigid, Cerridwen, Arianrhod, Grian, Aine, Melusine and many, many more

Whenever you have need of anything

Once in the Lunar Cycle

And better it be when the Moon is Full

You shall gather in a secret place

And worship the Spirit of Me

Who is the Queen of all Wise

When you gather

You shall be free

And you shall sing, dance, feast and make love

All in my presence

For mine is the ecstasy of the Spirit

And of moonlit joy upon this earth

For my Law is Love unto all beings

And the secret that opens the door

And mine is the cauldron of Cerridwen

Overflowing with Awen

And that is the Holy Grail of Immortality

I bring the knowledge of Spirit Eternal

And with death I bring peace, and freedom and reunion with those who have gone before

Behold: I am the Mother of All Things and my Love is poured upon this Earth

Hear the words of the Star Goddess

The dust of whose feet are the heavens

And her body encircles the Universe

I who am the beauty of the Green Earth and the White Moon among the Stars and the Mysteries of the Waters

I call upon your soul to arise and come unto me

For I am the Soul of Nature that brings life to this Universe

From me all things proceed

And unto me all things must return

Let my workshop be in the heart that rejoices, for behold – all acts of love and pleasure are my rituals

Let there be beauty and courage, power and compassion, honour and humility, mirth and reverence within you

And you, who seek to know me, know that all your seeking and yearning will mean nothing, unless you know this mystery

For if that which you seek, you find not within yourself, you will never find it without

I have been with you from the beginning, and I will be there at the end of your souls' journey.

THE REDE

Bide within the Law you must

In Perfect Love and Perfect Trust

Mind the Threefold Laws, you should

Three times bad, and three times good

Honour the Old Ones in deed and name

Let Love and Light be guides again

Merry Meet and Merry Part

Bright the Cheeks and Warm the Heart

These eight words the Rede fulfil

An ye harm none, do what ye will

An ye harm none, do what ye will

An ye harm none, do what ye will

THE DANCE OF SHADOWS AND LIGHT

Unrelenting light burns and blinds. Unmitigated darkness keeps us hidden and silent too long. We must have this glorious dance of dark and light to nurture ourselves, grow, extend, go within, rest, then move back out again. We are in and of this rhythm as surely as seed and sun and foal and flower.

What can I do?

When the clamour and rage gathers all around me

When my peace is frayed and tangled and I feel the war in the world seeping into me

What can I do when I see friends tumbling out old hatreds, writhing in the grip of fear, hating their cultures or hating the world

What can I do when I see the flashfire that is war burning the goodness from once-kind people?

I will go to the water and wash myself clean, and give thanks for the thirst that is quenched with its purity

I will turn my face to the sky and let my eyes fill with blue and feel the shapes of clouds pour into my mind

I will lay down heavy on the green grass and be held by the earth and the dirt and the clay and the deep growing world 'til my heartbeat eases

I will let the sunfire warm me, let my bones drink in the light, and I will bring me back to life

And then I will continue, to do the work, to love, to grow, to write the words, to seek the truths that live in the heart of life's mystery.

THE NATURAL CYCLES

Experiencing sadness, or anger, or any number of the opposite of 'up' feelings and situations do not make you less-than, or a failure in any way. There are times when we are summer, full and warm, golden beings of growth and light. And then, there are times when we are winter, more introverted and experiencing fear, or sadness, or pain. We vanish into ourselves to find the truth right at our core. In this life, we rise and we fall. To judge yourself less-than for having a natural cycle of experience and emotions is as futile as damning yourself for growing older each cycle of the sun. You will shine and you will grow dark at times. You will smile and you will cry. You will dance and at times you will curl inwards with pain. Both your descent and your rise are worthy, and can have honour, nobility, strength and lessons for you – and for others. We fall apart, we are rewoven, we die to things, we are reborn. This is the nature of everything that is. Why would you be separate to that natural cycle? Do your best. Be kind. And love not only others, but this self that you are for this fragment of time. Thou art magick.

SONG FOR OSTARA

I honour the maiden the mother the crone
I honour the wild ones, for they are my home
I honour the animals, the birds and the trees
I honour the awen, the imbas, the sidhe

I honour the maiden so wild and so free
She lives in my spirit, she lives in this seed
I honour the maiden, Grian of the sun
Take now my offering, so new life shall come

Ostara is stirring, her white hare runs free
She dances in fields, who flower as she
Moves through the meadow, the bush and the town
Ostara brings life, she wears nature's crown

Flora's beside her, Cernunnos and Herne
Ostara stirs brightly, the Horned One will learn
Of the power of Goddess; who kisses the land
We will drink in her milk, feel her white hand

Into your palm she presses this seed
You know of this secret, she asks you to heed
The lessons of priestess, of oak, birch and thorn
Of gum and of bush and of flowers reborn

You now have your task, a ritual, a vow

To bring back the life, and from your hands will flow

A season of springtime, of love and of kin

A warmth in the heart, for bliss reigns within

This seed is my love for the lady of earth

This seed is a journey to my own rebirth

This seed is my soul, my body, my heart

Now seed, bless this earth, of which I'm a part

Ostara she smiles, and Grian she is proud

Herne he leaps up, rebirth is allowed

Pan's pipes sing their song, of sweetness and mirth

And this is because

We have sewn the good earth

A MAGICKAL DEDICATION

The working of magick means adhering to certain natural laws. When we understand and work with them, our lives become harmonious, magickal, and we become who we were born to be: magnificent, magickal, free beings, whose choices create a better world and whose very existence is a blessing. You may wish to say to yourself:

I am free.

I harm none.

I seek no power over another.

I understand that what is created in love, creates a vibrational field of love. I understand that the opposite is also true.

Having established those natural laws, we may wish to look deeper into what walking the magickal path may bring us. We may wish to reconsider our promises to ourselves, and begin the process of replacing conditioning with a more evolved and compassionate, more magickal set of truths. Your magickal dedication may go something like this:

I learn of magick of my own free will, for the good of my own self, and for the highest good of all.

I work with the natural cycles and energies of the planet in ways that create a beautiful life.

I respect all life as sacred, and know that this earth and her inhabitants are sacred too.

I will honour the natural laws of creation, attraction and peace. I am now in the service of peace, love and highest good for all.

I respect and allow differences. I will not judge, but I will discern and choose freely.

I believe the world is best served by my becoming most truly my authentic self.

I thank the Universe, the God and the Goddess and myself for opening to me the wonders of magick.

Your soul is like a sun, bringing life to a million dreams, warmth to cold hearts, radiance where once dwelled shadows. Shine this day and be most blessed, dear friend.